ECOLOGY BEGINS AT HOME

Using the Power of Choice

Archie Duncanson

Illustrations by Roy Chadwick

Green Books

Contents

Contents

Part Three
Eco-Checklists for Individual and Household

This edition first published in 2004 by Green Books Ltd
Foxhole, Dartington, Totnes, Devon TQ9 6EB
edit@greenbooks.co.uk www.greenbooks.co.uk

First English edition: Ecology Begins at Home, 1989,
Saettfro Forlag, Stockholm, Sweden, ISBN 91 7328 7377

Swedish: Ekologi borjar hemma, 1995, Saettfro Forlag,
Stockholm, Sweden, ISBN 91 972626 0 9

Danish: Oekologi begynder hjemme, 2001, Borgen Vorlag,
translated by Otto Sigvaldi, ISBN 87 21 01294 6

Cover design by Rick Lawrence
samskara@onetel.com

Text printed by TJ International, Padstow, UK
on 100% recycled paper

ISBN 1 903998 45 X

Part One

I DECIDED TO DO SOMETHING ABOUT WORLD POLLUTION!

Tagliatelle from Italy

Sounds good, doesn't it? But for many people this means a steady flow of lorries carrying bulky noodles between factory and us—lorries which take up space on the roads and give off unhealthy exhaust fumes. Why do I pay for this long-haul trucking with all its pollution, when I could move my hand a few inches on the shelf and choose another brand made closer to home?

This book is about this and similar choices. It tells how I set about radically reducing the amount of pollution I create and the energy and raw materials I use up every day: my rubbish, the waste from my foods, my laundry, cleaning chemicals, etc. It tells how I looked for and found practical solutions to almost everything—things I could do in my own life, without waiting for governments or industry to act. It tells how I have succeeded, yet have not finished. It tells how working with my rubbish and other daily problems gave unexpected benefits: less dependency, a cheaper cost of living, better health, more creativity, joy, peace of mind and hope for the world.

Although you may not wish to do everything that is in this book, I hope it will get you active, too!

My Part in World Pollution

All the pollution in the world is caused by people. It is made up of my part, your part and each of our neighbours' parts, added together in thousands of towns, cities and villages around the world. Pollution from car exhausts, for example, is the sum of many trips—to work, to the shop, to school and to places of recreation—taken by millions of us each day, throughout the year. The coal, oil and nuclear power plants' pollution comes from meeting my needs, your needs, and all the other people's needs for heating, lighting, cooking, refrigeration, air-conditioning and other machines.

Oil spills—all of our responsibility, when we use oil.

Consider the oil spills off the coast of Brittany in 1978, Alaska in 1989, Spain in 2003, or any of those since: we blame the oil company, but is it not we who are paying them to engage in this dangerous work, to heat our homes and drive our cars? Each one of us can think that our part is so small, but it all adds up.

We have our shares, too, in the factories spewing smoke and dumping chemicals, when we buy their products. Their smoke is a little of mine, a little of yours, a little of all the other customers. For example, the frozen dinner I buy comes from a factory using lots of

World pollution—the whole is equal to the sum of the parts: mine, yours, and everyone else's.

energy, and more pollution is generated as it is transported along the road by diesel lorry. A share of that factory's energy and that lorry's smoke is mine.

If we look at every item we buy or consume, we will see that behind almost everything there is a factory, resources, energy and transportation—all causing pollution in different ways. Without realizing it, we are all party to this enormous world problem by simply living the way we normally do.

We can look at the enormity of the whole world's pollution problem and become discouraged, thinking "What difference can I make?"—and do nothing.

Or we can look at our share, which we have control over, take responsibility and say: "I am going to do something about it!"

My pollution . . . .
I'm doing something about it!

Other people's pollution

I decided to do something about it, and I started with my rubbish.

I Started with My Rubbish

Everybody knows the problems our daily rubbish causes for our local councils: where to put it, what to do with it. Some is buried (polluting the land); some is burned (polluting the air, and also the land where the ash is buried); some is cast out to sea. All of it must be collected and transported elsewhere—so there is pollution not only from the rubbish but from the lorries driving it around. Nobody really has a good, lasting solution for rubbish.

So I asked myself: "How can I reduce my rubbish?"

When you ask such a question, you get many ideas and answers. I began with the throwaway plastic drink bottles and aluminium cans, going over to returnable bottles and recycling the cans. This made a big dent in the amount of my rubbish. Then, seeing tin cans and glass jars in my rubbish, I gradually stopped buying preserved foods. Instead I bought more fresh and dried foods, which have little or no packaging. For example, instead of canned soup I made my own, with fresh vegetables, noodles and a bouillon cube.

ONE STEP AT A TIME

Next came wet rubbish. Acting on an idea I had read, I started a compost heap in my cellar. It didn't work very well the first time, but after a few experiments I got it going, moving it to my balcony where there was plenty of fresh air. All vegetable peelings, egg shells, coffee grounds, tea leaves, etc. now went under my sink for a week to begin fermenting, then into the compost box on the balcony of my flat. There it turned into earth again, which I used in my flower boxes and vegetable garden or gave away to friends for their gardens.

The rubbish was really getting smaller now. I began to look at every single thing I threw away, and ask myself if I couldn't avoid it. Newspapers at first went to recycling, but after noticing how little of the paper I read, I decided to buy it only on Sundays, and listen to the news on the radio instead.

All of these steps took several years of gradual change. I tackled one problem at a time, solved it and went on to the next. Month by month, the rubbish got smaller. Today my weekly rubbish is down to a single little bag weighing a few hundred grams, less than half a pound, for a single-person household. It is composed mostly of plastic bags. I am still looking for ways to eliminate them! My goal: zero rubbish.

HERE'S WHAT I DID TO REDUCE MY RUBBISH

- Fewer throwaway bottles and aluminium cans, mostly returnables.
- No paper plates, cups, serviettes, towels—I used cotton serviettes and towels.
- No aluminium foil or clingfilm—I covered leftovers with a plate or put them in a container with a lid.
- Fewer tin cans and glass jars—lots of fresh food instead.
- Recycled the newspaper, or didn't buy it.
- Composted all vegetable scraps (beginning with tea leaves under the bushes in the garden!).
- Began measuring my rubbish and jotting down my actions in a checklist. When I saw how much smaller it got, I knew I was on the right track!

My Rubbish for the Week:

Date	Number of Bags
Last week	///// ///
This week	////

My Food

I started to think about the food I eat. If we live on a farm or have a vegetable garden, we can go out and dig up fresh vegetables to cook and eat. No fertilizers or sprays are necessary, and the peelings can go on the compost. Chickens eat scraps from the household; other animals graze peacefully in the pasture, which they fertilize with their droppings. Fish in local waters live a free life on insects and plankton before we catch them. We eat what the earth gives us, and return the scraps to become new earth again, year after year, in an endless cycle.

In our modern society, things are not so simple. Much of our food is grown with chemicals, processed in factories, packaged in throwaway containers and transported long distances by lorry before we get it—each causing problems along the way. Farm animals do not live on food scraps and pasture grass but in crowded buildings, pens and cages, fed on imported food made from grains, maize, soybeans and fish; then they are transported long distances to slaughter and the meat processed in factories, packaged and transported to the shop. The earth suffers further from land

I pondered the long chain of events behind my food.

and water shortages, and from overfishing. These problems that come from the way we get our food are ruining the earth because they are so extensive, including most of what we eat, day after day.

I examined these sources of pollution in turn to understand them, then looked to see what I could do to eliminate them in my own life.

PROBLEMS FROM FOOD PRODUCTION

Farm Fertilizers and Chemicals
Chemicals in farming mean many things, but I think especially about these:

- Factories and raw materials are needed to produce the fertilizers—this means energy, smoke and chemical waste, including heavy metals in the waste.
- The fertilizers run off into the waters where they grow too much algae, destroy fish habitats and pollute groundwater.

I pondered the flow of farm chemicals: from chemical factory to farm to tractor to field to residue and run-off, and eventually into the water supply.

- Pesticides and weed killers are not good for our health, either as residues on our food or as run-off in the groundwater we drink; nor are they good for the health of the farmers and workers who handle them daily.

Factory Processing

Food processing requires a factory somewhere that uses energy, and creates smoke and waste. The food is first cooked, then cooled or dried, requiring much energy. All this is extra energy because the food must be heated again at home when we cook our meal. So a factory-prepared meal requires three steps (cooking and freezing at the factory, cooking at home) compared to only one when we cook something fresh at home.

Some factory processing examples:

- *Frozen peas*: boil, freeze, package
- *Parboiled or minute rice*: cook, dry with hot air, package
- *Instant mashed potatoes*: cook, mash, dry by heating
- *Cornflakes*: cook, mash, roll out, dry
- *Canned soup*: cook, cool, can
- *Instant coffee*: boil water, make coffee, dry by freezing
- *Dried soups*: boil water, make soup, dry by freezing

Since so much of our food requires three times the energy to prepare, it is no wonder the world burns so much energy today!

Energy

And how does energy pollute? Coal and oil power plants give off smoke, particles, and acids in the air, all of which harm lakes, forests, farmland and people's health. And like all burning, they give off the carbon dioxide that is causing global warming.

Nuclear plants have their own problems, leaving enormous quantities of radioactive wastes—all of which must be stored underground for thousands upon thousands of years. They also have accidents—truly dangerous accidents such as Chernobyl, that can kill directly or give cancer to hundreds of thousands of people and leave whole regions unsafe for living creatures for centuries or longer.

Fuels for energy (coal, oil, uranium) pollute where they are mined or drilled, then during their refinement, and then again during their transportation. They are in limited supply and thus a source of international conflict: the more energy we need, the greater the potential for conflict.

Packaging

A package begins with getting the raw materials: a mine for metal cans, an oil well for plastics, a sand quarry for glass and a forest for paper. Mining is a particularly dirty business, with daily run-off of chemicals used in the extraction process—the resulting metal is wasted on food and drink packages that are used once only then thrown away.

The simplicity of nature's package.

Package-making also requires energy: to melt the steel, the aluminium and the glass, to boil the oil for plastics and the wood pulp for paper. Making aluminium requires the most (enormous quantities), thus making our

All this is required to make a tin can: an iron mine, a steel plant, a can factory, a power plant, and transport in between.

aluminium drink cans the worst packaging of all from the point of view of energy usage. Even with recycling, the old package must be re-melted to make the new one.

Packaging also requires transportation: for example, iron ore to the steel mill, steel to the can factory and finished cans to the food processing plant.

Transportation
The long-distance transportation of food means lorries criss-crossing our cities and motorways filled with all that we eat every day. Very few foods come from the area in which we live: most come from more like 300 miles away, and some are transported 3,000 miles or more. Look at the labels, and you will see what I mean!

I realized that what I do when I purchase these items is pay for their shipping—and for the pollution from the lorries.

Worst of all are bulky items such as bread, cornflakes, pasta, biscuits and potato crisps. They take up lots of space in a lorry—the box contains mostly air!

A bag of rice is another matter—it takes up little space, and many meals can be prepared from it. Dried beans, nuts, seeds and straight spaghetti are also compact.

Factory Farming

Today's intensive animal farming means raising animals indoors in large buildings that require heating, air conditioning, and huge amounts of water for cleaning up. The animals eat pellet food made from grains, maize, soybeans, vegetable oil and fishmeal. Today, something like half of the world's farmland, grain and irrigation water, and a substantial portion of its energy, goes to feeding animals. To produce 1 kg of meat it takes 10 kgs of grain—grain which could feed ten times the number of people as the meat does, or more.

Factory farming: little land and labour used locally, but uses ten times the land, water and energy to grow animal feed somewhere else in the world.

Factory-farmed animals are also fed antibiotics regularly to prevent the diseases that come with overcrowding. These antibiotics create resistant bacteria. Further, the conditions under which the animals live is often harsh beyond words and entirely unworthy of kind human beings.

Land and Water Shortages

Deforestation. Forests are cut down to make farmland, causing many problems including soil erosion, landslides, flooding, lowered water tables and the extinction of animal and plant species, and even human cultures. This made me reflect on the choice between cutting down forest to graze cattle for my meat, and eating less meat.

Wetlands. Wetlands are drained to make more farmland, causing problems similar to those resulting from deforestation: soil loss, lowered water tables and loss of wildlife habitat.

Overgrazing. The demand for meat and the shortage of good farmland in the world puts pressure on people everywhere to overgraze on common or government-owned land. When land is overgrazed, the vegetation is slow to grow back the next year. As a result, the land is eroded by wind and water; the rain runs off too fast without seeping into the soil, causing floods, and the water table drops. Gradually, the earth turns to desert.

Over-irrigation. To make more farmland, governments fund huge water projects such as dams and redirected rivers to irrigate dry land and desert. These projects cause irreparable damage as they move water from one place to another. Redirected rivers cause lakes and deltas to dry up. Dams remove land from farming by filling up the valleys with water. Dams also prevent the natural seasonal irrigation and fertilization of the lowlands, requiring those areas to be artificially irrigated and fertilized. Artificially irrigated land becomes saltier with time, and eventually cannot be farmed, so all the energy and construction work that go into these giant water projects only help to produce food for a limited period.

I asked myself: "Is this worth destroying whole regions for?" And I reflected on my choice between a local winter vegetable and an imported one grown with precious water in the desert far away.

Overfishing

Overfishing means that more fish are caught than grow each year. When this occurs year after year, eventually none are left. Today, most of the world's major fishing banks are overfished. In addition, modern fishing methods are extremely inefficient and wasteful—more than half of the catch is thrown dead back into the sea because it is not the type of fish wanted.

I pondered the resources that go into the fishburger, shrimp, crab or lobster that I eat for lunch.

Fish farming attempts to solve the problem by raising fish in enclosures in a lake, river or sea, and, like factory farmed animals, feeding them with pellet food made largely of grains, maize and soybeans grown on land. Farmed fish are also fed antibiotics to prevent disease. Farmed salmon are fed a chemical to colour the meat pink. While fish farming can seem to be a solution to overfishing, it requires huge areas of land, water, chemicals and energy to grow the grains, so it solves one problem while creating others elsewhere.

GETTING MY FOOD WITH LESS HARM

Seeing all of these problems behind our daily food, I began looking for better alternatives: not theoretical or future solutions for how food could better be produced, but practical ways that I could get my foods without adding to the pollution and problems today.

Just as with my rubbish, I looked at one item at a time. I kept asking: "How can I get this without the transportation, without the processing, without the package, without the fertilizers? Without the deforestation, destruction of wetlands, overgrazing, irrigation, overfishing or factory farm?" Usually I couldn't solve all problems at once—it didn't matter, every step was a step in the right direction and I found new solutions all the time.

Here are some of the things I did. Your choices may be different.

Food Near to Home

When I became aware of the transportation problems, I began reading the labels and looking for alternatives nearer to home. Sometimes I didn't find any, so I ate something else instead, or made my own.

- I found out which breads were baked near my home and bought them, instead of the brands from 100 miles away. The same for cornflakes.

- I stopped buying kiwi fruit from far away and ate what was in season at home. In the winter I bought dried fruit, because it is compact.
- I never found tagliatelle produced nearby, so I ate straight spaghetti instead—one-tenth of the volume!
- I ate sprouts grown on my kitchen counter instead of lettuce from far away. Or I ate local cabbage in the winter.
- Potato crisps came from far away, so I bought peanuts instead—more compact—and made popcorn at home. A left-over boiled potato from the fridge, dipped in salt, also tasted good and had less fat!
- I cut down on imported biscuits and treated myself instead to fresh biscuits from a local bakery. Sometimes I baked my own.

Simple choices in the shop soon cut the transportation distances (or bulk volumes) of my food to a tenth, a twentieth or even a hundredth of what they were before. I was no fanatic, however, and sometimes ate my favourite potato crisps or bread—but as special treats, not regularly. It is the daily things which add up.

More Fresh Food

When I understood the true costs of processed food in terms of energy, packaging and pollution, I began leaving it on the shelf and buying fresh foods instead. I read the labels to see what was in things (soups, sauces, mixes, frozen dishes), then went home and made them myself.

- Instead of juice in the morning, I ate a fresh orange or a grapefruit—no processing, no package.
- I made my own soups from fresh ingredients: onion soup, tomato soup, noodle soup, cheese soup, celery soup, lettuce soup. You name it, I tried it!
- I baked a potato rather than buying frozen chips or making powdered mashed potatoes.
- I bought fresh fruits and vegetables that were in season (such as cabbage, cauliflower, carrots and apples during the winter) instead of frozen, canned and imported from distant lands.
- I bought some sun-dried fruits and vegetables—no processing, little packaging, and compact to transport.
- I boiled my own dried beans instead of buying tinned: mung beans, garbanzos, pintos, black beans, kidney beans, lentils—variety and taste for every occasion!
- I avoided meat substitutes such as soy sausages and vegetable pâté in my daily diet, since they require factories to produce. Instead I ate the beans directly or made my own hummus-like bean spread from left-over beans.
- For desert I made apple sauce at home. I dried and froze rhubarb from my garden.
- I stopped buying ice cream and ate frozen banana instead. I made sorbets or frozen yoghurt with my own berries and local fruit.

Looking in my cupboards today, I see an abundance of fresh and dried foods with which to start my dinner—hardly a tin, jar or carton—and know that I have come a long way.

Simpler Cooking, Simpler Meals

To keep it fun and practical, I simplified recipes and discovered ways to cook good tasty food with little effort. Often I cooked things in only one or two pots and enough for two nights at a time. I dared to be creative and cook without a cookbook—I trusted my own taste and smell. When I was in a big hurry, I made a quick soup of diced potatoes or red lentils that took ten minutes—no more than a frozen dinner, much fresher, and much healthier for the planet.

For each meal, I started by asking, "What shall it be tonight: rice, potato or pasta?" Then I added vegetables, beans, spices and a salad, or whatever I had on hand, to provide vitamins and taste. For example, I cooked up garbanzo or pinto beans with interesting herbs and spices and served them with rice.

A baked potato: simple to make and cooked only once. Together with cheese and a salad, a complete and healthy meal!

• I put fresh vegetables to steam directly on top of the rice, saving one pot to tend and wash up.

• I ate less fried food and more baked and stewed—healthier, and easier to cook.

• I put food on to simmer, like over a campfire, then let time do the work while I did other things.

• Many evenings I ate a hearty salad

as my main meal. Healthy for me, and no energy required from the earth.

- I sprinkled nuts or sunflower seeds on salads and hot dishes to give a chewy texture, nourishment and an interesting flavour.
- A simple dessert was often a piece of fruit in summer, or my own frozen and dried fruit in winter.
- I served plain yogurt for nourishment with vegetarian dishes or as a nourishing dessert, sprinkled with a little sugar.
- I learned to make a simple pie crust of flour and butter. Then I could make vegetable pies and quiches for my guests. I used the same pie bottom to make fruit pies for dessert.

With every step I ate more wholesomely, more tastily and with less effort. I did things simply: I let the food be itself and let time do the work. I used what I had on hand, I combined like an artist, and no two meals were ever the same.

Organically Grown Foods

To eliminate my share of the farm problems (fertilizers, chemicals, overcrowded factory farms and land and water shortages), I began looking for organically grown foods, produced locally, that do not pollute or harm as they are being grown. Some organically grown vegetables came from very far away, so I bought non-organic or ate something else instead—everything was a trade-off.

- I grew sprouts on my kitchen windowsill and tomatoes on my balcony. Later, I started my own small vegetable garden. Most organic foods cost more, but I saved so much money from buying less frozen and processed items, that I didn't mind. Besides, I got higher quality and supported the kind of agriculture in which I believed.

- I avoided genetically-modified (GM) foods because I questioned the wisdom of farmers taking unknown risks without thorough, long-term testing.

- I gradually switched over to a more vegetarian diet based on grains, potatoes, legumes, nuts, seeds, dairy, an occasional egg and a little fish, plus lots of fresh vegetables and fruit. For example, I ate pasta with steamed vegetables, butter and a little cheese or yogurt. Or I made tomato sauce for pasta as usual but without the meat. I made quiche with vegetables instead of ham or salmon. I got my protein from the grains complemented with seeds, nuts, beans and dairy products.

- I also ate less sugar, questioning the health of sugar in everything from breakfast cereal to yogurt and soft drinks, and the wisdom of using valuable land and water to grow sugar rather than food.

Today I get half or more of my foods more ecologically by shopping organic, choosing what I eat and growing a little of my own. I see my choices as an investment in my health and a more healthy world. I am still working on it, finding new choices that give both me and the earth the best I can, for the well-being of all.

HERE'S HOW I MEASURED MY PROGRESS

- *Food checklist.* I began a list of some of my new choices, with two columns: 'Old Choice' and 'New Choice', adding items as I tried them out.
- *Locally produced foods.* I kept a list of locally produced items that I found in the shops.
- *World map.* I traced a simple map of the world and wrote in some of the distant foods I bought. I crossed them off when I found closer substitutes.
- *Recipes and experiments notebook.* I started a notebook of my kitchen experiments to help me remember which recipes turned out best, what worked and what didn't.

My Drinks

To reduce my rubbish I had stopped buying drinks in throwaway cans and bottles, but after working with my food, I began to understand that there was more pollution behind a drink than just the can or bottle.

So I asked myself: "How are canned and bottled drinks made?" Here are the basic steps.

1. Grow the sugar, fruit and other flavouring ingredients on a farm (sugar-free soft drinks use synthetic sweeteners made in a chemical factory).

2. Make the packaging material:
   - Aluminium from a mine and a smelter factory
   - Plastic from an oil well and a refinery
   - Paper carton from a forest and a paper mill

3. Make the can, bottle or carton at a package factory.

4. Ship the cans, bottles or cartons to the bottling plant.

5. At the bottling plant:
   - Mix sugar, flavours, preservatives and other ingredients in water to make the drink.
   - Pasteurize by heating (many, but not all drinks).
   - Ferment (drinks such as yogurt, beer and wine).
   - Bottle, using the new package or a washed returnable

bottle (with bottle caps from another factory) and labels made using paints and inks from yet another factory.
• Pack in six-packs or shrink-wrap with plastic from another factory.

6. Load onto lorries, drive to a regional warehouse for storage; reload and drive to the local shop.

7. You or I purchase the drink and transport it home.

What a long and complex process for a single packaged drink! It attests to humanity's great skill in organization (getting so many people to work together for a single goal), but it also causes pollution problems every step of the way.

I pondered the energy, transportation and industrial waste behind a simple soft drink.

Comparing drinks to foods, I came to the conclusion that the farming problems (fertilizers, chemicals, irrigation, etc.) were usually small, at least for soft drinks which are mostly water, while the packaging, processing and transportation produced the majority of the pollution.

Bottled drinks are heavy, bulky items. If I had to import all my drinks for a year all at once in bottles or cans, imagine how many cases that would be. A lorryload, perhaps? Now consider if I drank nothing but tea, as many people in the world do, how much would I need for a year? Perhaps only a small carton—because the water does not have to be transported, only the flavouring!

So every time I drink tea, iced-tea, lemonade or plain water from the tap, I am saving part of a mine or oil well and refinery, a bottle factory and a brewery, and the transportation of all that liquid across town—the entire packaged drink process. I am being truly effective: the water flows to me in a pipe with no packaging, I add a little tea, sugar or flavouring (simple things to transport) and it is done!

Least polluting of all is plain tap water, which saves even the pollution produced in making the flavouring. So I began drinking plain water for lunch, carrying a bottle of tap water when travelling, and eating a fresh fruit instead of buying a bottle of fruit juice. When I really wanted fruit juice, I bought juice concentrate and mixed it at home, saving the transport of all the water.

My wish today is for every human on the planet to have what I have: access to clean, healthy water from the tap (or from a nearby stream or well). When I drink water from home, I am helping this come true, because some of the mines, factories and farms that pollute groundwater while making my packaged drinks need not exist anymore—not on my account, at least.

Drink choices	Lifecycle steps
Throwaway can:	mine, can factory, brewery, shop, home, rubbish
Recycleable can:	can factory, brewery, shop, home, recycle
Returnable bottle:	brewery, shop, home, return
Homemade drink:	shop, home
Water from the tap:	—

My Laundry

One day I saw an incredible amount of suds coming out of the washing machine, and understood all of a sudden why biologists were alarmed about chemicals in detergents: here were large quantities going down the drain from a single wash. I had always used somewhat less than the recommended dosage, to be economical, but now I became suspicious. For the first time, it occurred to me to find out for myself how much I needed, rather than rely on the manufacturer's general recommendation (which of necessity must cover the dirtiest laundry such as a car mechanic's workclothes, rather than my particular situation).

USING LESS

I experimented by cutting the dosage in half. The clothes got clean. I cut it in half again—the water still felt "slippery", and the laundry got clean. I continued in this way, and found that a heaped teaspoon, or even less, was enough for my laundry. I also discovered that cuffs and collars did not get really clean no matter how much detergent I

One heaped teaspoon
was enough!

used—they had to be scrubbed by hand. Using so little detergent I needed only one rinse cycle, not the four rinses that are standard on my machine. So I could use less rinse water and be finished in half the time. One kilogram of detergent powder now lasts me 2 years!

This is one of many experiences which taught me to find out things for myself by trial and error, rather than relying on authorities. More and more I rely on my own five senses plus my common sense. I know when my laundry is clean, by feel and smell, even though I only use one-tenth of the recommended amount.

And here, a desire to improve the environment has ended up saving me time and money as well!

There are many people experimenting all around us. We only have to listen to our friends and neighbours and read the newspapers to get ideas to try. We can then experiment, adapt, add a new twist, be creative and find our own novel way of doing something.

I experimented in reducing the amount of products I used all over my home. For example, I found that a paintbrush could be cleaned with a tiny spoonful of thinner, just enough to wet it, then washing it in washing-up liquid. I found that dishes required less soap if I used much less water, so I bought a plastic basin to wash up in, like when camping—one litre of washing-up liquid now lasts me two years! By treating all chemicals as valuable resources, I found ways to use less.

MILDER CHEMICALS

I also began looking for harmless substances that break down quickly in nature, so that even the small amount I used would be safe. For example, I bought laundry detergent without phosphate and chlorine. (If your city removes phosphates at its water treatment plant, it is still better to buy phosphate-free because you save the city from buying the special chemicals that are needed for removal, and the pollution from the production of those chemicals at the factory where they are made). I stopped using chlorine bleach entirely, hanging my clothes to bleach in the sun when I could. Instead of dry cleaning, I washed some things gently by hand and stopped buying clothes that I could not care for myself.

I discovered that many traditional cleaning substances are extremely mild and useful:

- *washing-up liquid:* this is my all-purpose cleaner for the whole house. I use it everywhere, including washing windows, floors, the bathroom and the car.
- *vinegar:* for when I wanted to kill bacteria in the toilet bowl, keep ants away and soak up odours in a room.
- *lemon juice:* for dissolving bathtub rust, cleaning brass and copper, and other uses.
- *bicarbonate of soda* (on a damp cloth or mixed with water): for cleaning the refrigerator, stained tea cups, and many other kitchen tools.
- *soda crystals* (sodium carbonate) (on a damp cloth or mixed with water): for really bad grease, such as in the

oven, and washing walls or woodwork before painting.
- *salt:* for wine stains and as an abrasive
- *alcohol:* for cleaning home electronics, tape recorder heads, and so on.
- *olive oil:* for polishing wood counters and keeping leather soft.

I found I could get by with these for almost everything, and they are now my basic household 'chemicals'—all come across by experimenting with something simple I had around.

Look in the market: shelf after shelf of detergents, soaps, special cleaners, sprays, polishes and abrasives—most of them harmful to our world (not to mention the factories that produce them). Do we really need them? Experiment, and you, like me, will find simpler, safer ways to keep your home, clothes (and car, if you have one) clean—with only a fraction of what you buy today!

HERE'S HOW I MEASURED MY PROGRESS

- *Purchase date.* I wrote the purchase date directly on the package whenever I bought a new box of detergent or household chemical, to see how long it lasted.
- *Inventory.* I began making a list of chemicals in my home—under the sink, in the cleaning cupboard, in the garage—with the two columns, 'Old Choice' and 'New Choice', then wrote in my new choices as I tried them out.

My Toiletries

I also began examining my toiletries and what I use to keep myself beautiful and clean. I stopped buying aerosol cans because of the energy needed to produce the can, and also the freon or other spray gas inside; and I switched to unbleached toilet paper to save a factory dumping chlorine into the water on my account. Knowing that everything I used meant factories, energy, packaging and transportation, I chose things more carefully and used them sparingly.

For example, I found that a bar of soap lasts two or three times as long as liquid hand soap (I always got too much of the liquid on my hand), and it leaves no plastic bottle to throw away. A shaving stick lasts many times longer than a tube or can of shaving cream, and it is packaged in paper. Examining things in this way and being careful not to use too much, I soon reduced my usage to perhaps a third of what it was.

Liquid soap goes down the drain, but a bar of soap gives just the right amount.

NOT USING AT ALL

But I went further. I began asking myself, "Do I need this item at all?" I thought of our ancestors, and wondered how they solved a particular need with no consumable resources, or virtually none (because such products were expensive or did not exist then). For example, a cloth handkerchief instead of paper tissues? Or cloth baby nappies instead of paper? What did they do without sunscreen lotion? Would a long-sleeved shirt and hat do just as well? Questions like these always gave me ideas—then it was only a matter trying them out.

When I switched from single-use to cloth items, I quickly discovered that they were easy to wash but no fun to iron. So I simply stopped ironing serviettes and handkerchiefs, stretching them on the line to dry and accepting a few wrinkles. Besides, these things gave me and my guests a feeling of luxury: isn't it at fine restaurants where they lay the table with a real tablecloth and cloth serviettes?

I also experimented by not using fabric softener. Fabric softener reduces static electricity on synthetics that are tumble-dried, by coating the fabric with a thin chemical. For synthetics, this is an overkill solution to a minor inconvenience, and for cottons it isn't needed at all.

MAKING MY OWN

Going further, I tried making some of my own toiletries with lemon, olive oil and other simple, natural ingredients that I had at home. I found recipes, then tried them out! Baking soda for deodorant, vinegar water for hair rinse! Believe it or not, I found that a little urine moistens skin and kills dandruff—the same chemical, urea, is found in most skin lotions under the name carbamide. For sunburns and mosquito bites, I took a leaf from my indoor aloe vera plant and squeezed the juice onto the skin, soothing it immediately.

Sometimes I also asked, "Is this item really good for my health?" A few years ago I cut down on soap when I read how it takes the natural oils out of the skin. The oil produces vitamin D and keeps our skin from drying out—why wash off our own oil, then rub lotions back on? I found that most of the time a daily shower with a scrubbing brush and a little soap under the arms got me clean—now I use soap or shampoo only when I truly need it. My senses tell me when.

My Home Energy

HEAT AND COOLING

I thought about the energy I use in my home. I grew up in an old Spanish house in Los Angeles, which had thick walls and lots of shrubbery and trees to shade the house and garden. My father taught us to keep the house shut on hot summer days—windows closed and curtains drawn—to retain the cool air from the night. In late afternoon when the sun went behind the hill, we opened up for the night, shutting again in the morning before the day got hot. Practically all homes in California had air conditioners, but our family never needed one, by simply closing the windows and curtains at the right time.

I read how trees and bushes near buildings slow down the wind and save considerable heat during the winter, even when they are 10 metres away. Ivy and other vines growing up the sides of buildings, I believe, provide a similar thermal blanket, in both summer and winter.

Trees and vines shaded our house from the sun in the summer, and slowed down the wind in the winter.

Each little leaf provides shade from the sun, and slows down the wind like the fur on an animal. So I planted bushes along the side wall of our building (not blocking any windows, which let in the warming sun) and a row of bushes along the street.

Knowing that the usage of heating fuel goes up about 5–10% for every degree centigrade that you raise the indoor temperature (for an air conditioner, the effect is similar but in the opposite direction), I often decided to put on a sweater rather than turn up the heat.

Shutting the windows, putting up quilts and curtains to keep out draughts, planting trees as a windbreak and putting on a sweater are old, simple solutions that cost almost nothing of me or the earth. Like thick-walled houses, they are extremely efficient and appeal to me because they use natural elements and natural laws, rather than relying on machines that use outside energy and must be kept repaired and run continuously.

NEW WAYS TO COOK

During an energy-saving campaign a few years ago, I read that the Swiss government encouraged citizens to boil the family breakfast eggs in steam rather than in water, to save importing oil that was expensive for the national economy. I tried steaming eggs: it worked, taking just a little longer than in water. Heating only one-tenth of the amount of water requires one-tenth of the heat, so the savings are major. I tried it with potatoes, and it worked just as well. So today I steam all my vegetables, cutting my energy to one-tenth of what it was and keeping the vitamins better, too!

From backpacking I had learned to cook on one burner, and to turn the burner off as soon as the food was boiling, letting it finish cooking and soaking up the water in its own time—slowly. After turning off the heat, I covered the pot with a towel to keep the heat in. Now I applied this trick at home. Some things, such as brown rice and large potatoes, need to simmer a while before shutting off the heat, and may need a few more minutes of heat toward the end after they have soaked up the water. (Dried beans should always simmer until well done.) Even so, I rarely have the burner on for more than 5 minutes at a time, and in this time I can often boil up two pots, such as rice and vegetables, one after the other. The secret is in letting time do the work. Left alone, nature soaks up water and heat at its own speed, without much energy.

Cook slowly with less water.
Let time do the work.

Experimenting further, I discovered that spaghetti or any other pasta does not need a huge pot of boiling water. It cooks very nicely in exactly enough water (just as we usually cook rice) if covered, brought to a boil, then left to soak up the water and heat without further heating. The secret is in covering the pot and turning off the heat just as it comes to a boil, and it saves half of the energy or more.

I also got in the habit of turning off the porridge shortly before it boiled, and the oven a little before the cake was done, to utilize the after-heat. Saving a few minutes of electricity or gas may seem small, but it all adds up over the month and the year!

Most of our cooking methods developed from cooking over wood fires, over thousands of years. People did not need to conserve energy, so it was alright to have a pot of hot water boiling on the wood stove in case guests arrive, and to cook pasta in huge pots full of boiling water. Today we need to rethink and invent new ways that fit our equipment and our times. Try these methods, experiment, and maybe you will find even more efficient ways!

HERE'S WHAT I DID TO CONSERVE COOKING ENERGY

- I always used a lid when I boiled food to keep the heat in.
- I steamed eggs, potatoes and vegetables, rather than boiling them.
- I cooked pasta like rice in exactly the needed amount of water.
- I turned off the burner when the food came to a boil, covered the pot with a towel and let the food 'steep'.
- I thawed frozen food overnight in the fridge or on the

counter before cooking, saving half the energy to heat and cook.

- I utilized after-heat in the oven, turning it off a little before the food was done.
- I measured exactly the amount of water I needed in the electric kettle—no more.
- When possible, I cooked my meal in one pot instead of two (for example, putting vegetables on top of potatoes or rice as they cooked), saving both energy and washing up!

USING ELECTRICITY AND HOT WATER WITH CARE

After the kitchen stove, I went through the other energy-using appliances in my home one by one, eventually cutting my electricity usage in half and my hot water by much more.

I pondered how I could save electricity. Switching off lights, electronics and appliances is simple; the only difficulty being that they seem so insignificant! I used to think, "One little light doesn't matter", until I realized that turning off one of the two lamps lit in a room meant halving the energy. Gradually I got in the habit of turning off all the lights when I left the room, and my computer or stereo when I was done for the day or evening.

Every time I turned off a light or appliance, I smiled and thought, "Now they can turn down the generator at the power plant a wee bit and save a little coal, oil, uranium or whatever they use!" I also thought: "Archie, would you leave a tap running when you weren't using the water?"

HERE'S WHAT I DID FOR ELECTRICITY AND HOT WATER

- I turned off my refrigerator during the winter and used my cool pantry instead.
- I set my freezer to the recommended temperature (no colder). I shut it off entirely during part of the year.
- I washed at 40°C and saved an extra load by mixing whites, coloureds and synthetics into one load.
- I dried clothes on a line outdoors in summer and on a rack indoors in winter, rather than use the dryer.
- I bought clothes that don't need to be ironed such as knits, flannels, patterned cloth and pure cotton that can be stretched on the line.
- I turned off my TV and stereo using the power switch on the unit (rather than the remote) to save the standby current.
- I shut down my computer when I finished working at home and at work. At lunchtime, I shut off the screen.
- I disconnected battery chargers and converters when not in use. I got an extension cord with a switch to make it easier.
- I cut out baths and shortened my showers.
- I rinsed off the dishes with cold water. I wiped off really greasy plates with old newspaper or a used paper towel.
- I washed up the dishes in a small basin of hot water instead of the sink (not under running hot water!).
- I switched off lights, thinking "Each little bit counts!"

HERE'S HOW I MEASURED MY PROGRESS

- *Bills.* I jotted down my electricity bill and compared it to the previous one, seeing how it decreased over the years.
- *Checklist.* I began a list of energy users in my home—cooker, refrigerator, freezer, washer, dryer, shower, etc.—with the two columns 'Old Choice' and 'New Choice', then wrote in my new conservation measures as I put them into practice.

My Water

We all see on the news how people on our planet suffer from two major water problems: pollution and shortages. Water is a circulating global resource and plays an important part in the globalized economy, so water is everyone's concern. I began to see how my share of the problems comes not only from the water I use at home but from the water involved in the foods I eat and the goods I buy, which are produced all over the world.

WATER POLLUTION

Major sources of water pollution are sewage, industrial chemicals, mining, landfills, military operations and agricultural run-off.

Sewage. A sewage treatment plant is a living process which, like a compost heap, must be kept safe from substances that harm it, such as medicines (especially antibiotics and hormones), garden chemicals, solvents, paints, plastics and phosphates. Even biodegradable substances such as washing-up liquid and fat from foods create a problem when there is so much of it concentrated in the sewage outlet of a city. The less I put down my drain, the better.

Industrial chemicals, mining and landfills. I realised I could reduce my share by reducing how many manufactured items I bought. For example, fresh foods save the chemicals that are used to make packaging. Home-made drinks save the mining for aluminium used in the cans. Not buying disposable paper cups, plates and serviettes saves the chlorine used to manufacture them.

Agricultural run-off. Problems come from heavy use of chemical fertilizers, which cause algal blooms, and from biocides which harm human drinking water as well as animal, bird, insect and plant life. I could reduce my share by buying organic, by growing my own and by simply not eating and drinking particularly harmful farm products.

HERE'S WHAT I DID TO KEEP THE WATER CLEAN

- Used less of everything (for example detergent and washing-up liquid), so less went down the drain.
- Used mild chemicals and gardened without poisons.
- Took strong chemicals, paints, batteries, etc. to the recycling centre, and medicines back to the chemist.
- Used no fabric softener, no drain cleaner, no phosphates.
- Put fat in the rubbish, not down the drain (also saves a clogged drain).
- Bought organic foods and grew sprouts on my kitchen worktop.
- Bought less tinned food and canned drinks because of the water pollution from mines.

WATER SHORTAGE

Shortage of fresh water is due primarily to the growth of the earth's population and to society's industrialization (including agriculture with its factory farms and fish farms), both of which are still increasing rapidly.

Irrigation is by far the biggest user of water. Perhaps half of irrigation water worldwide is used for growing the grains, maize and soybeans to feed factory-farmed animals and farmed fish. The other half grows food that is eaten directly by people.

I pondered the amount of water I used every day.

Industry is the second major user, with water used to wash and clean in the making of almost everything from paper products, clothes and processed foods to home electronics. Power plants in themselves use huge quantities to cool their electricity generators.

I began reducing my water usage at home, but more importantly, reducing my use of manufactured goods and foods that cause water to be used elsewhere.

HERE'S HOW I SAVED WATER IN MY HOME

- Washed and rinsed dishes in a smaller basin.
- Flushed the toilet less often.
- Took shorter showers.
- Wore shirts and trousers several days, saving washing so often. I hung them to air each night.

- Mixed whites, coloureds and synthetics in the laundry to make a full load.
- Skipped the prewash and sometimes some of the rinse cycles.
- Watered plants with rinse water from my sprouts (full of nutrients) and sometimes with my washing-up water (a little washing-up liquid does no harm).

HERE'S HOW I SAVED WATER IN THE GARDEN

- Watered at night, so the water could soak into the ground and not evaporate so much.
- Watered directly under each plant, rather than using a sprinkler which spreads the water far and wide.
- Covered beds with cloth, or each plant with an over-turned glass jar, to hold the moisture while the plants got rooted.
- Planted hardy plants that fit the climate and needed little or no watering.
- Watered seldom but well—so the roots grow deep and can survive.

HERE'S HOW I SAVED WATER ELSEWHERE IN THE WORLD

- Cut my purchases of disposable products, especially paper, that require a lot of water in the making (for example, paper towels and the newspaper!).
- Cut my electricity so that less water was needed for power plant cooling.
- Ate less meat, poultry, fish and eggs, because feed grain

requires so much water to grow (lots of it is irrigation water) and animal farm buildings require so much water to clean.

MY DAILY HOUSEHOLD WATER NEEDS

My household usage is around 50–100 litres per day—about the minimal need per person estimated by the United Nations for basic modern needs with running water and flush toilets. A mature industrial society lifestyle with washing machine, dishwasher, cars, etc. uses many times this amount. People who must walk to obtain their water use, of course, much, much less.

My daily water needs:

Drinking	2–5 litres
Cooking	2–5 litres
Washing dishes and hands	5–10 litres
Shower, bath	30 litres
Laundry	5 litres (1 load per week)
Toilet	25 litres
Garden	Variable (during summer only)
Total approx.	**70 litres per day**

My Clothes and Possessions

Our ancestors lived on earth for millions of years with all of their homes, tools and possessions disappearing back into the earth, save for a few bits of pottery, stone and metal, and some of their bones. Only recently have we manufactured artifacts of such a nature and in such quantity that they have become a problem, in both their manufacturing and their disposal after use.

To give myself an idea of the magnitude of my needs, I began to list things that I might buy during my lifetime: 80 pairs of shoes, 20 jackets, 5 bicycles, 5 television sets, 5 stereos, radios or CD players, 5 cameras, 10 telephones, 10 computers, 3 each of stoves, refrigerators and freezers, 5 cars (with 5 new batteries and 5 sets of new tyres for each car)—and so on.

This was enough to give me the picture, and I did not like what I saw. Like a good camper, I wanted to leave the campsite clean when my life was over. So now I asked myself, "How can I reduce the energy and chemicals needed to make my possessions and the rubbish resulting from them?" I began with recycling.

I began to list the things I might buy during my lifetime . . .

RECYCLING

Recycling means that raw materials are used again. For example, rather than digging up new aluminium ore, aluminium cans are collected and sent back to the factory. Collecting an aluminium can means one less shovelful of ore dug up, one less shovelful refined with electricity and chemicals. Recycling thus saves dirty mining and energy, as well as landfill space.

I found out what could be recycled in my city: glass, newspapers, food packages, aluminium drink cans, and other metals.

I also found out what to do with things that could not be recycled and that might cause problems if they were put into the rubbish bin and sent to a landfill, put down the sewer, or otherwise got out into the natural environment:

- Medicines (for example antibiotics and hormones, which affect all living creatures)
- Batteries containing mercury and cadmium (no safe processes are known for recovering these metals)
- Car batteries containing lead and acid
- Light bulbs (some contain a small amount of lead, others mercury)
- Car and lorry tyres (a fire hazard in a landfill)
- Paints and chemicals (for example, from car and garden)
- Electronics such as computers and stereos

Our city had a recycling centre to collect and sort such things separately. Medicines, paints, oils and some chemicals that we handed in were destroyed by burning. Old cars were partially dismantled and the steel recycled. Electronics, batteries, light bulbs, tyres and car batteries were sent to special depots to be stored, since no recycling processes existed for them. Some were sent abroad for storage. By visiting the recycling centre, I did my part.

MEETING MY NEEDS WITH LESS ENERGY AND WASTE

But I didn't stop there. Knowing that everything I bought meant manufacturing pollution and rubbish, I looked for ways to cut down the quantity of things I needed for a happy life.

First, I considered quality. I had been raised with the habit of being very economical and buying most things cheap. But when I thought about it, I realized that an expensive, good quality item requires approximately the same energy, chemicals, transport and other resources to make as a cheap item, but it will last a lot longer, so is better for the earth. For example, a quality wood table can become my great-grandchildren's antique and last a hundred years, whilst a chipboard table, which used the same energy and caused the same amount of pollution in its manufacture, may last only 10 years. So a table (or whatever) that can live to be a hundred is ten times as efficient for the earth.

Second, I realized that my home was so full of 'stuff' that I didn't have any room to put it! My home was like a pipeline that is full: any new thing that I brought in the front door meant that something else had to be pushed out of the back door!

I also remembered Gandhi's reflection: that man's material needs are finite and can be met, but that man's desire is unlimited. Desire is a powerful force in our world: the desire for more, for new, for change, etc. If I follow my desires blindly, my life results in full wardrobes and attics that eventually cause much material pollution and rubbish. Since there truly is no limit to what my mind

Do I really
need this?

can imagine, I understood that I must impose my own limits. Limiting myself, like eating only what my body needs, brings its own health and quiet satisfaction, while following desire—for example, the desire to own things—leads to continuous dissatisfaction and a never-ending search for the grass that is always greener somewhere else.

I saw that I needed a new ethic, a new way of thinking. Instead of asking if I could afford something, I began asking myself, "Do I really need this item? Where will I put it? How often will I use it? Is it going to give me true satisfaction, or just a kick for the moment? Will it help the world, or just be a waste cleanup problem for the people of the future?"

Instead of looking for 'a good deal', I looked for quality and what I truly wanted. Instead of trying to be 'in fashion', I sought to be ecologically efficient and satisfied.

Seeing how my impulsive desires led me to buy things that I later regretted, I got into the habit of going home and 'sleeping on it' before making a decision.

I repaired and took care of things. I patched clothes, sewed on buttons and sewed in new zips.

When I could, I rented or borrowed things rather than buying them. Sometimes I made do with what I had. Other times, I bought second-hand or made things of my own, often from 'recycled' materials I had collected that others had thrown out. A lot of my furniture is hand-me-down or home-made. These possessions required no extra resources of the earth—they were already made.

Third, I asked myself what makes me happy, and began noticing my state of mind. I quickly came to realize that my happiness mostly had to do with people and little to do with things (otherwise, the rich would be happier than the poor, wouldn't they?).

I discovered that I was a creative being, and that much of my happiness came from expressing myself, in creating things—actual things or dinners or social events or whatever—for myself and for others. It was the creativity and the social interaction, not the physical circumstances, that gave the joy, so it didn't matter if I were rich or poor, I could find joy either way. And I thought, "We need a lot of creativity to create the happy world that we want without ruining the earth!" Without it, our many possessions will be worthless anyway.

With creativity you can be happy, whether you have a lot or a little.

Finding out how to be happy with fewer material things is all the more important today because the less fortunate in the world always imitate and copy the lifestyle of the rich, just as our parents did and their parents before them. This has resulted in the problems we face in the world today, which many of us are doing our best to understand and solve.

HERE'S WHAT ELSE I DID

- I was satisfied with a used computer, sufficient for my needs.
- I bought quality that lasts, and repaired things to make them last.
- I didn't buy clothes that needed dry cleaning, nor toys and tools that required a continuous supply of chemicals or batteries.
- I didn't subscribe to the daily newspaper because I read so little of it, and I unsubscribed from magazines that were sent to me free that I didn't read.

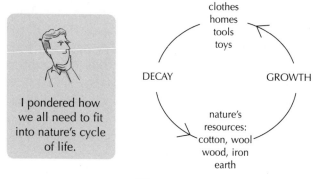

I pondered how we all need to fit into nature's cycle of life.

clothes
homes
tools
toys

DECAY   GROWTH

nature's
resources:
cotton, wool
wood, iron
earth

My Gardens

I have three gardens, all of which I try to care for simply and naturally, without any chemicals or machines and with little water.

I have a balcony, made into a little garden where the birds come to visit all year long. It is mostly flowers, but I have strawberries too, and a redcurrant bush on a stem, as a little tree—lots of berries in July! The earth comes from my own compost.

My community garden is an allotment rented from the city, 3 miles away. It is 10 x 10 metres, and I grow healthy vegetables, potatoes, fruits and flowers, and enjoy picnic lunches there. I garden without chemicals and cover the ground with straw and grass to keep the moisture in and the weeds down. By composting, I never need to buy anything except seeds in the spring. We also sometimes get straw that they throw out from the local stable. The wood for my fence, windbreak and storage box is all 'second-hand' that others have thrown away—as are my garden chair and table. Ordinarily I do not turn the earth, wanting to leave the insects and worms in peace, so I pull up weeds by hand. I have many herbs and perennials that always attract the bees. After the harvest, I collect seeds for myself then let all the stalks stand through the winter because they give food and shelter to so much life—besides, they look pretty standing in the frost and snow, and remind me of the summer that has been.

In addition to herbs, flowers and vegetables, I also have berry bushes in my garden: raspberries, currants and gooseberries. I eat these in season and make jams for the winter, as well as freeze some of them whole.

My indoor garden graces the windowsills with greenery of many shapes and hues, some grown by me from seeds. I use compost as fertilizer, and now and then water them with washing-up water. If they get too many insects on them, I put them under the shower or spray them with soapy water!

Many forms of life share the same space, in silent cooperation.

All of my gardens show a little bit of the wild in them. I tame them a bit, to please my human sense of order, but deep down I know that it is Life itself that rules and does the growing there, not me.

HERE'S WHAT I DID

- Fertilized with compost from my kitchen, a little of my own urine on occasion (diluted with water) and nettle-soaked water.
- Left a brush pile for hedgehogs to make their home.
- Planted perennials, rose bushes, shrubs, parsley, chives and herbs that come back each year, making the garden as self-sustaining as possible.
- Selected hardy varieties that grew well in my climate.
- Covered vegetable beds with breathable cloth to protect from wind and cold: either non-woven or fine nylon netting (old curtains bought second-hand do well!).
- Used hand tools whenever I could, giving myself exercise with useful work and saving one machine in the garden plus the use of another in the gym.

My Car

When it came to the car, I had problems: I was addicted! I blamed it on my upbringing in Los Angeles (when public transport hardly existed), and kept on with my habit. I tried several times to take the bus to work, but it never lasted more than a day. It was as bad as quitting smoking, or worse!

An endless queue of traffic: when I am stressed, nature is too.

What finally got me out of the habit was the example of a friend, who rode the bus to work and her bike to the local shops. She had a car, but hardly ever drove it, out of concern for the environment and for her own exercise.

Inspired, I began following her example of taking the bus to work, and found many unexpected benefits. First, I saved lots of money. Second, my conscience felt immeasurably better—now I was doing what I felt was right instead of just talking about it. Third, car repairs were much easier: I could do many myself since the daily pressure to have the car was off. Fourth, instead of sitting in traffic and swearing at all the other drivers for being out on the roads, I got time to read the newspaper or a book, to prepare for the day's work, and just to ponder life. It took longer, but my mornings were very peaceful.

Transport choice	Relative pollution
Car	1
Car pool with 2 people	$\frac{1}{2}$
Motorcycle	$\frac{1}{4}$
Scooter, Light motorcycle	$\frac{1}{8}$
Bus	$\frac{1}{16}$
Train	$\frac{1}{32}$
Bicycle	0
Walk	0

GETTING MORE EXERCISE

A further benefit to me was getting more exercise. I believe we humans need our exercise, just like other animals. Just as hens, lambs, cows and pigs on the farm become stressed and sick when they are shut in, so too do we become sick when we shut ourselves in day after day in our high-rise buildings, homes, offices, cars, hospitals, classrooms, etc., with little movement.

A bike ride or walk instead of the car (for example, at lunchtime) changes all of this. That little ride or walk is effective in three ways: it gives exercise and health, keeps the air clean, and saves petrol for future generations.

Eureka!

So I began walking and biking—to the shop, to my garden plot, to the library, everywhere. This gave me peaceful time to relax, as well as daily exercise and stimulation. While others took their dogs for a walk, I walked myself to the shop!

Most of my creative thoughts come to me while I am walking, biking or running.

I have found that many of my most creative thoughts (including lots of the ideas in this book) come to me while I am in motion: walking, biking or running. I also get ideas while riding the bus or train and looking out the window, so I always carry a little notebook to jot them down. These are times of peacefulness, like on a boat cruise, when the mind is free to relax and ponder while the world takes care of itself.

I still kept my car for the sense of freedom it gave, but I treated fuel like other valuable household chemicals and used it sparingly. Whenever I thought of taking the car I asked myself, "How many litres of fuel will I burn up for this trip?" and then pictured that number of milk cartons filled with petrol and burning with ugly black smoke in the air. Other times I thought, "Today seems like a good day for a bike ride. I think I'll save that litre of petrol for a rainy day."

MY NEXT CAR

My next car, if I ever need one, will probably be small, use little fuel and most likely be second-hand. Small means less of all the resources required for manufacturing, smaller tyres and batteries to replace, and less scrap for the landfill at the end of its life. Little fuel means fewer oil spills, less air pollution and less carbon dioxide.

A clean electric car might be good for the local air, but still runs on electricity from a power plant burning oil somewhere else!

Some problems from cars can only be reduced by driving and travelling less: traffic, noise, accidents, roads and parking spaces.

Even if I buy another car, I will still walk more and drive less. I will still save money, get exercise and drive only one-tenth of what I had done before. My vision: clean, quiet, friendly streets like the ones I grew up in, for all to enjoy.

My Recreation

Until a few years ago I was bothered by my car usage. For example, to go jogging I drove several miles to find a quiet lane. To go camping I drove fifty miles south of town for the weekend. Nowadays I jog right out of my front door and over to the nearest lane, or just around the neighbourhood. I camp on this side of town or bike to a nearby park for a picnic, without using the car at all. These small shifts in destination made my enjoyment efficient, rather than being a drain on the world's resources.

I started thinking about all the chemicals involved in taking photos, and the photos that I never looked at which were lying in boxes in my wardrobe. I decided to keep a diary instead, and record my impressions in words—a few little notes bring a whole scene back to mind. I illustrate with postcards, cut-outs from tourist brochures, an occasional photograph and letters from friends. These books tell my story and remind me of all that I have experienced, at little cost to the earth.

I always used to fly when my son and I went backpacking each year in the mountains to the north. One year we took the train instead, and never flew again. It took a little longer, but we got to see the whole country pass by slowly, at a pace we could take in: forest, farms, rivers, churches, old cottages, animals grazing and the mountain tops in the distance, dark purple. The chairs were comfortable, the rhythmic sound of the clickety-clacks was relaxing, and while I read, my son explored the train. In the restaurant car there was a view from every table, and we could eat or just sit and have a cup of coffee. And, sleeping on the train is always an adventure, especially for kids—where will we wake up in the morning?

Sun-dried parsley, tomatoes and strawberries—fun to make, fun to eat.

Taking the train, like taking a boat, riding a bicycle or using one's own two feet, gets you somewhere and you enjoy yourself at the same time. There is a simple efficiency here: doing two things at once. Similarly, working in my vegetable garden has become an enjoyable pastime as well as a contribution to my food.

Some people, I have noticed, are experts at this, taking every opportunity for enjoying the small things in life and making little celebrations out of everything—for creating happiness, quite simply, in daily life. This too is a kind of efficiency, which goes far beyond large-scale industry and costs the earth nothing. These people are teaching us something of great value, if we will watch and find out what they do.

In this spirit, I began organizing group activities such as picnics, walks and dinners. One year we had a weekly cooking group where we tried new recipes and learned from each other. Other years I went to local study groups for folk dancing, drawing, vegetarian cooking and later led some myself. These were all low resource, high participation, fun-generating activities.

The more I looked, the more I found ways to live, have fun, stay healthy and add to the good of the earth—all at the same time, without polluting or causing problems. This is the art of gentle living.

My Thinking

IMMEDIATE SOLUTIONS

I have long been a procrastinator. One day, in self-disgust, I made myself solve a problem right now, today, this minute—instead of putting it off to a better time (when I worked out the best way to do it, when I felt like it, when I had the right tools, when I could get help, and so on). Much to my surprise, I worked out a way to take care of the problem with what I had on hand, with no help and in very little time. It might not have been the best solution I could think of, but it was done—and it was done now.

I have since learned that for almost every problem there exists an immediate solution. It is just a matter of seeing it or finding it.

An example: one winter I was thinking about the heating costs for the apartment complex where I live, feeling discouraged because in order to do anything, I would have to go to the steering committee and get involved. And any action such as improved insulation would take years to implement. "This is a problem about which the individual can do nothing", I thought to myself. But as soon as I said that, I realized that no one was stopping me from turning down the thermostat in my flat, so I did, and put on a sweater. It was done in two minutes—immediate action!

Another time, when I was teaching, I saw paper towels in the cloakroom and thought: "They should use cloth hand towels, like they do at Southside School." I dried my hands while complaining to myself, then it occurred to me: no one is forcing me to use these paper towels. I could carry a handkerchief for the purpose, if I were really serious and didn't just want to complain. Or I could let my hands dry in the air, or pat them lightly on my trousers, as my father sometimes used to do. Since then I quite simply ignore the hot-air blow dryers in public conveniences and feel good, rather than complaining to myself and feeling bad every time I see one. I have found a solution which works for me.

When it was dinner time and I didn't know what to cook, instead of going out grudgingly (requiring both time and perhaps use of the car), I decided to work something out with what I had at home. I almost always ended up eating well, and this was when I was most inventive and free in my cooking.

Our main motorway into town had been getting more and more congested in morning rush hour, so that the buses were often standing still. The problem worsened for two years or more—the people who rode the buses were furious, but no one could work out what to do. Investment funds to build more roads were lacking, campaigns to get motorists to ride public transport were known to be hopeless, and so on. Then one day it was solved overnight, at no cost. The buses were simply given permission to drive on the hard shoulder of the road, bypassing all the standing cars and giving people on the buses, at least, a quick ride into town.

GIVING MYSELF HOPE

When I tried to solve the whole world's problems all by myself, I ended up unhappy and blamed others for not caring or not doing enough. I learned that it is better to look at the problems I could do something about in my own life. I did not have to try to change my colleagues, my children, my parents, my teachers, or my friends: it was enough if I worked on my own daily habits, at least at first.

When I acted and saw results—for example that my rubbish was getting smaller—then I had hope. If I tried and sometimes failed, with a little encouragement I could go on and look for other ways.

I let others be. I realized that I had come this far because of my own concern and desire for a better world, with a carrot rather than a stick. I believed that others would do likewise, in their own time and at their own pace, when the time was right for them. So I let my son be with his normal teenage habits, as long as he put the food scraps on the compost!

You can change the world!

I used to think, "It is so hard to change the world", until I realized that when I had changed myself, I had already changed the world.

STRESS, PEACE, HAPPINESS AND SATISFACTION

Stress, it seems to me, is the disease of our times. And when we get stressed, we stress nature, too. In fact, I believe our stress is a primary cause of the stress in the environment today. For example, consider how my desire for cheap food affects the animals on the farm—the hens, pigs, calves and cows. I press the farmer for lower prices, the farmer presses the animals. I take the car instead of the bike, use the clothes dryer instead of the sun, eat frozen meals instead of home-cooked, all requiring extra energy and resulting in pollution—because I feel this thing called stress.

All of that changes in an instant when I recognize my power of choice, that I am in fact the boss in my own life. I learned that just as I could choose milder chemicals in place of stronger ones, so could I choose peaceful activities and thoughts in place of stressful ones, if I reflected a little, experimented and practised. I could almost always figure out a new way to do what was needed that was more harmonious, or fun. And even when I couldn't change the circumstances, I could always choose a different attitude, which made everything look different—and less stressful. For example:

Ecology Begins at Home

Stressful activity or attitude	Peaceful alternative that I could choose instead
✗ Watch TV violence and news	♥ Walk in the park, sit by the water
✗ Read of corruption, war, injustice and misery in the world	♥ Listen to music, read an inspiring book with wise words
✗ Complain, accuse	♥ Take action, encourage others
✗ Blame others, blame myself	♥ Accept. "They are doing their best and I am doing my best"
✗ Try to do things "perfectly"	♥ Think "This is good enough", "I am good enough"
✗ Try to do too much	♥ Do the most important task

A friend of mine told me that the most valuable thing in life was our meetings with others, and that to miss an opportunity for a meeting with a friend or loved one was to miss out on a bit of life's richness. She is right, I think. All this rushing about misses the point of life: to be here enjoying it all together —this place, this setting, the animals, the flowers, the people, the wind, the water, the morning and the evening skies.

When I listen to my heart, I know what I truly want: a peaceful, healthy world shared with my fellow humans and other creatures. It is when I forget where I am, what I have and who is here with me that I become dissatisfied or afraid and the rat race begins. Who will stop the wheel turning, if not me? When, if not now?

My Results

Sometimes I thought, "Do I want token changes, or do I want to change the world?" Reducing my pollution by 10% was not enough for me—I wanted to be rid of it altogether, and soon!

DARING TO THINK BIG

How? In order to make big changes, I had to dare to think big. I challenged myself to try to cut my pollution to a third, a quarter, a fifth—a fraction of what it was. When I had succeeded, I could then try again to cut it to a third or quarter of that—another big reduction. Then I had left only a small fraction of what I began with, and the world—my part of it at least—was almost clean.

Setting my goals high made me think new, creative thoughts about things which I never would have thought of, if I were only looking for small reductions. For example, if I asked how I could reduce my car pollution by 10%, I might think of driving slower or getting a tune-up. This doesn't change the world very much, and without results, I might soon have given up. But when I asked instead, "How can I cut my car pollution to a tenth of what it is today", I saw immediately that it was a difficult problem: I must think up something entirely new, something clever. My mind went to work with fantasy, logic, imagination—everything I had—and gave me many ideas to try out. I may not have achieved my goal at first, perhaps I only got down to a third of what it is today, but that was good enough, I had made a good start. I was then in a much better position than if I had only aimed for small benefits. Later I could go another major step, and perhaps achieve my original goal.

My Pollution Inventory Today

Fraction left of original usage

Rubbish: A little bag each week — $1/20$

Food: few cans and jars, lots of organically grown and most in season from within the region where I live — $1/10$

Laundry, **Toiletries** and **Home Chemicals**: a few bottles per year — $1/10$

Home Energy:
- Heating down to ¾ of my original usage
- Cooking to ¼, refrigerator to ½, freezer to ½
- The washing machine to ½, dryer to almost zero
- Lighting and electronics to ½
- Hot water to ⅓

$1/2$

Car and **Recreation**: bus to work, bike to the store, train for vacations and save my car for rainy days. — $1/10$

My Total Pollution Before: — 1

My Total Pollution Today: — $1/10$

Next Year? — $1/20?$

The Choice is Ours

Governments, industry, farmers, scientists, ordinary people like you and I—all of us caught in self-interest, complexity, confusion, blame. All talk—no action. Helplessness. The house is burning down and we argue about who should pay the firemen, or how to put it out. Dear friend, do not get caught in all this blame! It is better to act before the house burns down.

World pollution problems begin in our own minds and our own homes. We can solve them here too. It is here we have the power to act, here that each one of us can make a difference, here that we can change things today

We have a problem, so let's do something about it! We each have our power of choice—and all our intelligence, common sense, creativity, courage and will. We have our passion for beauty, our sense of right and wrong, our belief in a meaningful life, and our perseverance. Let's use them now! We can take one thing at a time in our own lives and improve upon it, see results, feel satisfied and help others. We can find our own solutions, rely on our common sense, help invent new ways to live more gently on this planet. And we can start today.

One day I looked at the world's pollution, thought about my share in it and decided to do something about it. I started with my rubbish, and it has changed my life. Where do you want to start? The choice is yours. In the second part of this book I have set out all sorts of ideas that will help you on your way. Good luck!

Part Two

PRACTICAL TOOLS FOR A SUSTAINABLE LIFE

Composting Basics
Cooking With Very Little Energy
Simple Meals
Easy Home-made Drinks
Simple Beauty at Home
Household Cleaners

Composting Basics

Compost happens!

Composting is simple! It occurs of its own accord everywhere—in the forest, in the lawn, under the flowers, bushes and weeds. Big pieces crumble into smaller pieces and are eaten up by insects and animals. Insects, microbes, fungi and worms break down the cell walls. Water is released and evaporates to the air, until all that's left is a rich, crumbly mixture.

A compost heap may be in the garden or courtyard, in a cellar or garage, indoors or on a balcony. It may be warm (40–60°C) or cold (outdoor temperature). You can use a wormery, a compost bin, or just a plain compost heap: nature has many different breakdown agents that thrive in different conditions.

Composting is easy. One way is to layer 'greens' (vegetable scraps, lawn clippings, plants etc.) with 'browns' (scrunched-up paper, eggboxes etc.) that soak up the moisture. It needs air and moisture (if the compost is too wet it will smell, and if it's too dry it won't work). It also needs heat: you should insulate to keep the temperature above freezing during the winter (otherwise the compost-ing process will stop until spring).

All organic matter can be composted, but meat and fish may not be suitable for your composting method—check with your council on local regulations, as to whether a sealed bin is required. You can grind up branches and woody parts in a shredder, but should otherwise not put them in the compost (they take too long to break down).

It usually takes between two to six months for kitchen waste to turn into compost, and you can accelerate the process by turning the mixture. Garden compost with leaves and grass only takes longer.

Potential problems: flies—sprinkle a layer of soil or sawdust over the heap; rodents—keep them out with sheet metal or steel netting, or use a compost bin.

The best way to learn the art of composting is to visit someone who has a compost heap. Then you'll see how much fun it is!

Cooking with Very Little Energy

With these methods you can cook on a fraction of the gas and electricity that you use today, and save money into the bargain! Adapt, experiment and refine them to fit your cooking needs.

COOKING PASTA WITH MINIMUM WATER

- Place the pasta in a pot that has a tight-fitting lid and add water:
  - For spaghetti and other dry pasta: about 300ml water per 100g pasta.
  - For fresh pasta: about 200ml water per 100g pasta
- Bring to a boil, stirring as the pasta softens so that it does not stick. If necessary, add water so that the pasta is completely covered by water.
- Turn off the heat and cover loosely with a towel to keep the heat in. Be careful the towel doesn't burn!
- Ready after 10 minutes or so—the normal time.

Ideally, the pasta is perfectly cooked and there is only a little water left over in the pot at the end. With this gentle method, pasta does not overcook and the timing is not so critical. With practice you will learn how much water you need, and how to cook it for a small pot or for a big party and with different kinds of pasta.

COOKING SLOWLY ON AFTER-HEAT

- Bring the rice, beans, soup, potatoes or whatever to boil in a covered pot, turn down the heat and let it simmer, as usual.
- Before it is done (5 to 15 minutes before, depending on your stove) turn off the heat entirely, cover loosely with a kitchen towel to keep the heat in, and let it finish cooking using its own heat.
- For porridge, couscous and foods made with milk: turn off the heat entirely shortly before it boils, to keep it from boiling over.
- Be careful the towel doesn't burn!

With this gentle method, vegetables are still firm, fish does not get tough, and milk does not burn. With practice you will learn how early you can turn off the heat. If the food is not done, bring to a boil again, turn off the heat and wait a few minutes more.

COOKING IN ONE POT INSTEAD OF TWO

You can steam vegetables (or fish or tofu) on top of rice, pasta or potatoes, in the same pot:

- Bring the rice or potatoes to the boil in a covered pot, turn down the heat and let it simmer a few minutes (say 5 minutes), as usual.
- Add your vegetable (broccoli, cauliflower, carrots, green beans or whatever) directly on top, put on the lid,

bring to a boil again and finish cooking (turning off the heat before it is done to utilize the after-heat, as usual).

This method also works with pasta, with soft vegetables such as spinach or courgette slices on top. Pasta only needs 8–10 minutes cooking time, so the vegetable must be one that cooks in this time, too.

This method saves using a second burner and a second pot, and the washing-up!

POT WARMERS

I used a towel to insulate a pot on the stove after turning off the burner because it was simple and quick. Here are two other ways that hold the heat even better.

- Pot cosy: Make an insulator for smallish pots by taking a tea cosy and cutting open the seam on one end so that it can fit down over the pot handle, which sticks out.
- I use the pot cosy or a towel after I've served the food, too, to keep the pot warm on the table or on the stove.
- Cookbox: Take a large carton or wooden box and insulate with anything (even crumpled up newspapers work), leaving plenty of room for the pot to be placed in the centre. Make an insulated lid for the box, 3–5 cm (1–2 inches) thick or more. An old styrofoam cooler, big enough for your usual pot, may work perfectly.

Simple Meals

A few basic skills can go a long way toward making cooking easy, creative and fun—as well as making you less dependent on the shop and special manufactured ingredients. Here are some of my most useful base recipes, each of which can be modified in a thousand ways. If you also learn the basics of baking bread, you will be set for an independent, creative life of more personal and healthy cooking!

Sprouts: soak beans or seeds overnight, then rinse twice daily until done (3–4 days). Each kind tastes different: mung beans, alfalfa, radish . . .

Basic soup or stew: Fry a chopped onion in oil, add water and chopped vegetables, potatoes, dried lentils, beans or peas, salt and spices to taste. Add milk or cheese to give a thicker, heartier taste and increased nourishment. Add miso or a bouillon cube for more salt and flavour.

Miso soup made with leeks, lettuce or bean sprouts is a light, simple, delicate dish!

Basic pie crust: 250g flour, 125 g butter, pinch of salt. 1 egg (optional). Mix together with your fingers in a pie dish, adding a spoonful of water if too dry, then press out to line the bottom and sides. Bake at 200°C till it begins to dry and brown, about 10–12 minutes. Then add filling and bake again until the filling is cooked (about 20–30 minutes, feel with a fork). I always use wholemeal flour—more healthy, and has a nice nutty taste!

Quiche filling: mix 4 eggs + 400 ml milk and thinly sliced vegetables.

Dessert pie filling: berries or sliced fruit and sugar. Variation: brown sugar.

Basic biscuit: 200g flour, 200g butter, 180g sugar. Optional: dark chocolate chips, chopped nuts. Mix with your fingers. Form into small balls and place on oiled baking tray. Bake at 200°C about 15 minutes or until beginning to brown or they smell done!

Simple frozen fruit dessert: Approximately 200g fresh or frozen berries or sliced soft fresh fruit, 200g yogurt, sour cream, cream or crême fraiche and about 50g sugar. Mix with a fork, mashing the fruit. Adjust sugar to the tartness of the fruit by taste, then freeze. Let soften a little before serving.

Easy Home-made Drinks

You can make many drinks simply and easily yourself, instead of buying them and adding to the world's pollution.

These will get you started, then you can go even further if you find it fun (for example, some people make their own fermented drinks).

Simple Favourites: iced tea, lemonade, lemon water (slice of organic lemon in water). Fill your drink bottle at home and take it with you!

Helen's Mineral Water Powder: ¼ teaspoon each of sodium (or potassium) bicarbonate and citric acid in a glass of water, or 1 teaspoon each of the same in a litre of water.

Robert's Sport Drink Energy Powder: 1 teaspoon citric acid, ½ teaspoon ascorbic acid, about 80g sugar (adjust to taste). To make into a drink, add 1 litre water or take about 1 heaped tbsp per cup.

Caffeine Drink: Make tea or coffee or save the leftovers from your teapot and put in a bottle in the refrigerator to drink cold. Making your own drink saves the pollution involved in making a canned caffeine drink.

Apple or Fruit Soak: Wash and chop the fruit (seeds, peelings and all). Pour boiling water over and let stand in a cool place for 2 days. Strain, add sugar to taste, bottle and store in the fridge. Keeps for a week.

Sesame or Soy Milk: Sesame milk is easy to make: blend sesame seeds in water. To make soy milk, boil 200 ml soy flour in 1 litre water, whisking while it simmers for a few minutes—optionally add honey or sugar for taste. Even easier, and with the same nutritional value, is to sprinkle sesame seeds on muesli, porridge and salads, and to use soybeans as the base of a main dish.

Simple Beauty at Home

Try some of these simple methods that our ancestors discovered many years ago, or do without, or invent your own ways of being beautiful more naturally!

Hair rinse: a spoonful of vinegar or lemon juice in a litre of water.

Dandruff cures: rub coconut oil into scalp, then cover with steaming hot towel; or rub a little urine into scalp and let it sit overnight (it doesn't smell—urea is in most skin creams under the name carbamide, look on the labels!); or rub bicarbonate of soda into scalp, let sit a while, then rinse.

Deodorant: pat bicarbonate of soda under the arms (can turn white blouses slightly yellow with time).

Face cleaner, astringent: lemon juice or alcohol for oily skin.

Face packs: egg yolk (let it dry on your face), honey or mashed ripe banana mixed with a little sunflower oil (rich in vitamins!).

Face rubs: olive oil or other vegetable oil or mashed avocado for dry skin; lemon or fresh cut potato for oily skin.

For shaping hair: comb soft drink or beer into hair; dries quickly, holds the shape.

Lipstick: beet or berry juice for colour, lip balm or vegetable oil or beeswax for moisture (you can mix oil in beeswax to make it softer).

Household Cleaners

Here's how easily you can clean without the need for a hundred speciality products, using only simple things that you have around the home.

BASIC MILD HOME CLEANERS

Washing-up liquid: *(mild)* For general cleaning of kitchen, bathroom, tile, floors, doors, windows. I often add a squirt of vinegar, which helps to cut grease.

Vinegar: *(antiseptic, cuts grease, removes odours)* With washing-up liquid, for toilet bowl, windows. By itself to remove odour. (see Odours in the following section, 'Alternatives for Special Purposes').

Bicarbonate of soda: *(mild, cuts grease, removes odours)* Use on a damp cloth or mixed with water for cleaning the refrigerator, stained tea cups, glass, pans and many other kitchen tools. Wash and let it sit for a while then wipe clean.

Salt: *(mild, antiseptic, abrasive, absorbent)* For scrubbing stuck food, cleaning a breadboard, soaking up a wine stain and many other uses.

Sodium carbonate (soda crystals): *(strong, cuts grease, removes odours)* For tough spots like oven and for washing walls and woodwork before painting. Use on a damp cloth, or mix with water as per directions on the packet.

MILD OILS AND PAINTS

Olive oil: For polishing wood and making leather soft.

Linseed oil: For preserving outdoor wood and as a base paint to seal the pores before painting any wood.

ALTERNATIVES FOR SPECIAL PURPOSES

Bathroom scent: Broken pine needles, fresh flowers, fresh cut citrus fruit, fresh mint or other herbs.

Bleaching: Strong camomile tea—smells good! Hang clothes to dry in the sun. Use detergent with the bleaching agent percarbonate (<u>never</u> perborate or chlorine).

Brass, copper: Lemon juice, tomato ketchup or vinegar (let sit a while).

Burnt pan: Let soak—time does the work (soda or bicarbonate of soda helps).

Car wash: Washing-up liquid.

Car engine: soda (Keep soda off the car paint!).

Drains: Try a coat-hanger wire, use a plunger, or unscrew the pipework underneath the sink and clean it out.

Dry cleaning: Wash by hand instead. Use 'nature's dry-clean': hang clothes in the cool night air.

Fleas: Try fennel, rosemary or rue in pet food.

Lime deposits, bathtub rust: Vinegar, lemon juice (both acidic).

Odours: Let a pan of vinegar sit overnight in the car, room or cupboard that smells (for example, of smoke). For odours in the refrigerator, wash with bicarbonate of soda.

Silver: Soda and a small piece of aluminium foil in water (let it sit for a while). Do not use for silver that has a blackened engraving!

Waterproofing shoes: Vaseline, olive oil, beeswax, candle wax.

Wardrobe: Lavender, cedar chips, juniper.

Windows: Warm water with a little washing-up liquid and vinegar.

Woollens: Washing-up liquid.

AVOIDING STRONG CHEMICALS

I learned to make mild alternatives to these, and to keep them all out of children's reach! Most strong chemicals are harmful to humans, as well as to plants and animals when they come out into the drain water.

Ammonia: Use vinegar, lemon juice or washing-up liquid instead to cut grease and disinfect. Use soda crystals instead to wash walls.

Chlorine: Chlorine in the drain water harms all life as well as the ozone shield. Use vinegar instead to disinfect and percarbonate to bleach.

Perborate: *(bleaching agent in laundry and dishwasher detergent)* Choose a detergent with percarbonate instead.

Dishwasher detergent: Strongly alkaline—can burn a child's mouth and is not good for nature in the waste water. If you hand rinse before putting them in and run the dishwasher before the food dries hard on the dishes, much less is needed. Experiment and find out!

Acetone: *(spot remover, dry cleaning solvent)* Harmful to inhale and destroys the ozone layer. I stopped using these. I tried a little washing-up liquid on a grease spot, and if that didn't work, I let the small spots be. (A friend stitches a little flower over a spot!)

Paint thinner: Clean the brush carefully on newspaper, then use the absolute minimum amount of thinner to wet the brush, then wash in washing-up liquid. When painting several coats, put the brush in a jar filled with water, to save cleaning in between.

Part Three

ECO-CHECKLISTS FOR INDIVIDUAL AND HOUSEHOLD

Use the eco-checklists on the following pages to help you get started and work systematically. Keep track of your progress by simply checking off the sample actions as you do them.

These are not meant to be complete or exclusive, so add your own actions and ignore any that are not relevant for you. The first topic, Measuring Methods, gives pointers on ways to quantify your results.

The Eco-Checklists included are:

Measuring Methods
Rubbish
Food
Household Chemicals
Toiletries
Energy
Personal Resources
Local Choices
Savings from Ecological Choices
Resource and Pollution Inventory

Measuring Methods

Here are some of the ways I found to help make my results visible, so that I knew when I was succeeding, and by how much. Adapt freely to your needs and invent your own special ways to count success!

MEASURING BOTTLED DRINKS

Count the number of bottled and canned drinks that you buy and also note the cost, since bottled drinks are expensive and are often a large part of a food bill.

My drinks for the week:

Date	No. of Bottles / Cans
This week	///// ///
Later week	////

You can use this method of measuring to count many different frequently used items: tinned and frozen foods, washloads per week, newspapers purchased per week, etc. For less frequently used items, it is better to write down the purchase dates.

HOW LONG THINGS LAST

To see how long things last, you can write down the purchase date and size of the package when you buy the item. The next time you buy the item, fill in the next purchase column and count how many months have passed.

My purchases:

	Purchase Date	Package Size	Next Purchase Date	How long it lasted
Washing detergent	_____	_____	_____	_____
Shampoo	_____	_____	_____	_____

Note: I also write the purchase date on the package itself, which is even easier, but having a list gives me a record to refer back to later on.

MEASURING RESOURCES WITH BILLS

Bills can give you a good overall picture of your resource usage and tell you how much effect all your actions add up to. Make your own table for the important resources that you use and want to follow up! You can also include food if you want to, since almost all processed food is expensive (partly because of the packaging), so that a lower food bill indicates less factory-made and thus less resource-intensive foods.

My Bills:

Date	Quantity	Cost	Notes
Car Fuel			
———	———	———	———————
Electricity			
———	———	———	———————
Natural Gas			
———	———	———	———————
Oil, Wood or Coal			
———	———	———	———————
Water			
———	———	———	———————

After a few months you can make a graph or bar chart showing your bills month by month and follow the trends!

MEASURING SUSTAINABLE TRANSPORT

You can measure your overall car use by your miles driven and your petrol bills. Below is another way to measure: it is more immediate and highlights participation by all members of a household. To the extent that it includes walking and biking, it also gives a measure of exercise.

Journeys by Sustainable Means of Transport:
(Bike rides, walks, bus, rides with a friend, skate, paddle, row . . .)

	Adult 1	Adult 2	Child 1	Child 2	Child 3	Fuel saved (litres)
Jan	///	////	//		///	12
Feb	////	///	///	/////	//	17
Mar	. . .					

Count your 'sustainable journeys' in daily life using the table above, putting a slash for each bike ride to the shop, etc. Count 1 litre per trip, unless you have better info. Give yourself a pat on the back for every litre of fuel that you save. Keep in mind that it is about creating better air and better health—not a bad conscience. Instead, enjoy the thought that for every low-pollution trip you make, the air is a little bit cleaner and your health a little bit better than it otherwise would have been!

Keep a notebook in your car and record each fuel purchase so you can see how long it lasted (like with laundry detergent!).

MEASURING HOLIDAY TRANSPORT

Each time you travel, record your trip, means of travel and the estimated fuel consumed for it. The fewer total miles travelled, the better. The fewer air and car miles the better, the more train and bus miles instead the better.

My Holiday Trips:

Date	Destination	Miles travelled		Fuel used*
		By Car / Aeroplane	By Bus / Train / Ship	
29 June	Manchester		150	5 litres
10 Oct	Nairobi	6000		1000
_____	_____	_____	_____	_____
_____	_____	_____	_____	_____
_____	_____	_____	_____	_____
Total	All Trips	_____	_____	_____

* You can count 1 litre of fuel for every 6 car or aeroplane miles, every 30 bus miles and every 60 train or ship miles. For a car, the fuel estimate (1 litre for every 6 miles) can be divided among all the passengers in the car.

Rubbish Checklist

Here's how easily you can reduce your rubbish by 80% or more. Check off items as you do them and write in your own actions!

Instead of disposables:

❒ Cotton table serviettes

❒ Cloth dishrags to wipe up spills instead of paper towels

❒ Cover leftovers with a plate instead of aluminium foil or clingfilm

❒ Long-lasting cups and glasses, instead of throwaways, for parties and picnics

❒ _____

Lots of fresh food (without the packaging):

❒ Fresh orange instead of packaged orange juice for breakfast

❒ Fresh quartered potatoes in the oven instead of frozen chips

❒ Fresh vegetables instead of canned casseroles and pasta sauces

❒ Fresh fruit instead of packaged ice cream, pies and biscuits

❒ Home preserved or dried fruit instead of canned fruit

❒ _____

Rubbish Checklist

Other:

- ❐ Recycle the newspaper or don't buy it
- ❐ Drinks in returnable bottles or homemade
- ❐ Sign up to the Mailing Preference Service which takes your name off junk mail databases, and put a sign "No Advertisements, Please!" over the mailbox
- ❐ _____

Composting:

At home, on your balcony or with friends and neighbours who have composts or gardens that can make use of fresh compost!

- ❐ Tea leaves and coffee grounds
- ❐ Kitchen vegetable matter
- ❐ Later, possibly meat and fish scraps, if your bin is sealed and the location is suitable (check with your local council on what is allowed and in what type of bin)
- ❐ Garden rubbish

You can measure your rubbish for a week using a slash or "x" each time you throw out a bag. Measure again later and note the results.

My Rubbish for the Week:

Date	Number of Bags
Now	///// ///
Later	////

Food Checklist

Here's how you can cut pollution and other problems from your food and drink, support wholesome farming and give yourself the best at the same time.

Farm Chemicals

☐ Ordinary potatoes   **>**   organic potatoes
☐ Ordinary fruit & veg   **>**   organic
☐ Bananas (pesticides)   **>**   stop buying or buy less often

Processing *(energy, chemical preservatives and packaging)*

☐ Frozen carrots   **>**   fresh carrots
☐ Tinned tomatoes   **>**   fresh tomatoes, in season
☐ Tinned fruit for dessert   **>**   fresh fruit in season
☐ Instant coffee, tea   **>**   brewed coffee, tea
☐ Olives in a jar   **>**   buy less often
☐ Frozen dinners   **>**   home-made
☐ Instant mashed potato   **>**   home-made
☐ _____   **>**   _____

Food Checklist

Long-haul diesel lorrying *(and air transport)*

❑ Bread from another town   > local bread, bake your own
                         sometimes

❑ Potato crisps   > peanuts (compact)

❑ Apples from abroad   > local apples

❑ Distant lettuces   > local lettuce in-season,
                         sprouts, cabbages

❑ _____   > _____

Canned or bottled drinks *(mine, energy, oil, chemicals, waste)*

❑ Bottled soft drinks   > tap water

❑ Bottled fruit juice   > eat a fresh fruit

❑ Energy drinks   > make your own

❑ _____   > _____

Land and water shortage and animal suffering *(intensive animal and fish farming, irrigation, deforestation, etc.)*

❑ Eggs from caged chickens > free range eggs, fewer eggs

❑ Lots of meat, large servings > vegetarian meals, small
                         meat portions

❑ Lunch meats such as sliced ham, salami, beef
                         > cheese, avocado, tahini,
                         peanut butter

❑ Canned tuna   > garbanzo beans in
                         casseroles, salads

❑ _____   > _____

Household Chemicals Checklist

Here's how easily you can halve your usage and step by step switch over to milder chemicals for home, car and garden. Check off items as you do them and write in your own actions!

❑ **Detergent**   100ml or more > 1–2 teaspoons
❑   with phosphates > without phosphates
❑ **Bleaching**   every wash > every third wash
❑   with chlorine > with percarbonate
❑ **Fabric softener**   100ml > none at all
❑ **Washing-up liquid** big squirt > a little squirt
                 fill sink with water > wash in a small basin
❑ **Dishwasher powder**
             1 tablespoon/tablet > rinse carefully, ½ tbsp/tablet
❑   with phosphates > without phosphates
                   with chlorine > with percarbonate
❑ **Disinfect bathroom**
             chlorine, ammonia > vinegar, washing-up liquid
❑ **Bath rust**   special products > vinegar or lemon juice
❑ **Solvent to clean paintbrush**
                   1 cup solvent > 1 teaspoon
❑ **Car wash**   solvents > washing-up liquid
❑ **Garden furniture**
               wood preservers > linseed oil
❑ **Burnt pan** special cleansers > water: let soak for 1 hour

Toiletries Checklist

Here's how easily you can halve your resources for personal hygiene. Check off items as you do them and write in your own choices!

☐ **Hand soap**   liquid dispenser > bar of soap
                         big squirt > little squirt
☐ **Shampoo**   a palmful > half as much
                     twice a week > once a week
☐ **Deodorant**   regularly > a touch for parties
☐ **Toothpaste**   a long string > half as much
☐ **Toilet paper** bleached, printed > unbleached, plain
☐ **Shaving cream**   aerosol can > shaving stick
☐ **Hair shaper**   hair spray > soft drink or beer
☐ **Drying hands at work**
             paper towel, air dryer > cloth handkerchief
☐ **Guest towels**   paper > cloth
☐ **Cleaning up spills** paper towel > dishrag, newspaper
                                        or serviette
☐ **Sun protection** sunscreen oils > long-sleeved shirt, hat
☐ _____   _____ > _____

Many small, daily amounts add up to bottles and tubes saved per year! As with reducing rubbish, you can replace many single-use, disposable products with permanent items that last.

Energy Checklist

Here's how easily you can halve your energy usage, so that oil, coal and nuclear power plants can use less fuel or be closed. Add other machines and appliances that use energy. Check off items as you do them, add items and write in your own actions!

❑ **Shower (hot water)** 15 minutes > 5 minutes
❑ **Washer**   90°C (hot) > 40–60°C (warm)
❑ **Dryer**   always use > use when necessary
                                      (hang dry otherwise)
❑ **Dishwasher**   heat dry > dry without heat
❑ **Refrigerator**   coldest > least cold setting
❑ **Refrigerator** on all year round > use a cool pantry or
                                        balcony in winter
❑ **Freezer** coldest: -24°C (-10°F) > -18°C (-0°F)
❑ **Freezer**   on all year round > turn off for 4 months
❑ **Stove**   boil without a lid > with a lid
❑ **Stove**   "lots of water" > minimum water (pasta)
❑ **Stove** boil vegetables in water to cover > steam veg. in
               minimum water (also potatoes & eggs)
❑ **Stove**   burner on all the time > turn off before done,
                              use after-heat

Energy Checklist

☐ **Lights**   2 lamps lit > 1 lamp lit

☐ **Computer**   on all the time > shut down after use

☐ **TV, Hi-Fi, Radios, Battery chargers** stand-by mode uses
    electricity > unplug or push Power Off on the TV

☐ _____ _____ > _____

☐ _____ _____ > _____

☐ _____ _____ > _____

☐ _____ _____ > _____

You can also keep a list of your energy bills, jotting down
the energy consumption and cost each time it comes.

Personal Resources Checklist

With this list you can keep track of resources that are your own responsibility, not the household's. Measure first, filling in the first column, then ask "How can this be halved?" and try out new habits. On a later date, measure again, filling in the second column and compare. Modify the table to include the resources that are under your control.

Measurement Date:	Date 1	Date 2
Hot water		
Shower, minutes/day	_____	_____
Washing dishes, litres/day	_____	_____
Washing clothes, loads/week	_____	_____
Car wash, washes/month	_____	_____
Energy		
TV and computer, hours on/day (measure for 1 or 2 days)	_____	_____
Car fuel, litres/week	_____	_____
Clothes dryer, minutes per week	_____	_____
Air travel, km or hours per year (record the destination, date and distance)	_____	_____
_____	_____	_____
_____	_____	_____

Personal Resources Checklist

Measurement Date:	Date 1	Date 2
Food		
Meat, fish, fowl, meals per week (a slash for each meal)	_____	_____
Soft drinks per week (a slash for each packaged drink)	_____	_____
Other		
Shampoo, bottles purchased (record the dates)	_____	_____
Batteries, per week (a slash for each battery)	_____	_____
Film (or printer ink) purchases (record the dates)	_____	_____
Magazines/newspapers per week (a slash for each)	_____	_____
_____	_____	_____
_____	_____	_____
_____	_____	_____
_____	_____	_____
_____	_____	_____

Local Choices Checklist

Use this list to find out some of your local choices and to share with family and friends. Fill in applicable items and adapt for your own needs!

- ☐ Our nearest recycling centre is at _____
- ☐ We take computers and electronic equipment to _____
- ☐ We take paints, medicines, batteries and dangerous chemicals to _____
- ☐ Second-hand shops where we can buy and donate are located at _____
- ☐ Water hardness in our area is _____ (soft, medium or hard: soft water requires less detergent)

Environmentally friendly cleaning brands we can buy are:

- ☐ Washing detergent _____
- ☐ Dishwasher detergent _____
- ☐ (other items) _____
- ☐ _____

- ☐ Locally baked bread brands are _____

Local Choices Checklist

Nearest factory location for frequent food and drink brands are:

- ❐ Soft drinks_____
- ❐ Breakfast cereal, cornflakes, muesli_____
- ❐ Macaroni or other pasta _____
- ❐ Biscuits, crackers_____
- ❐ Potato crisps _____
- ❐ Other bulky food _____

Savings from Ecological Choices

Fill in the blanks to estimate savings from new choices that you make and see what you save. Change the number/week and add other items freely—these are just examples! You can also look at your food bills.

- ❒ Rechargeable batteries instead of ordinary, 4/week saves
    4 x ____(price)= £_____ /week
- ❒ Homemade soft drinks or water, 2 bottles of 1.5 litres/week saves 2 x ____(price) = £_____/week
- ❒ Homemade popcorn or crisps, __ packages/week saves ___ x ____= £____ /week
- ❒ An apple or an orange instead of a canned drink, 4/week saves 4 x ____= £_____/week
- ❒ Natural yogurt plus fruit juice instead of single-serving packages with fruit and a lot of sugar, 1 litre/week saves £_____ /week
- ❒ Something reusable instead of paper towels, 2 rolls/week saves 2 x ____= £_____/week
- ❒ A plate over the leftovers instead of clingfilm or aluminium foil, 1 roll/month saves £_____ /month
- ❒ Cloth table serviettes instead of paper, 1 package/month saves £_____
- ❒ Washing-up liquid instead of window cleaner spray, 1 bottle/month saves £_____
- ❒ Bar soap instead of liquid, 1/month saves £_____ /month

Savings from Ecological Choices

- ☐ Shampoo/bath gel, use half the usual amount, saves ½ x £_____per bottle x ___ bottles/yr = £_____/year
- ☐ Homemade biscuits, 2 packages/week saves 2 x ____ = £_____ /week
- ☐ Home-made soup instead of dried/canned (4 serving package), once a week saves £_____ /week
- ☐ Home baked potato wedges instead of frozen chips, 0.5kg/week saves £_____ /week
- ☐ Salt, spices, butter instead of packaged sauce, 1 pkg/week saves £_____/week
- ☐ Herbal tea, pick it in nature or in the garden, 1 pkg/month saves £_____/month
- ☐ Fruit or berries, hand-picked in nature or in the garden, 1 pkg/week saves £_____ /week
- ☐ Local cabbage or sprouts instead of far-away lettuce during the winter, 1 head/week saves £_____ /week
- ☐ Radio or TV instead of the evening newspaper, twice a week saves 2 x ____= £_____ /week
- ☐ Second-hand furniture, for example 1 table or chest of drawers saves £_____ (estimate the cost of new table, etc, less cost of used)
- ☐ Second-hand clothing, for example, a winter coat, saves at least £_____ (estimate cost of new minus used)
- ☐ Repair a zip or worn elbow in a coat or sweater instead of buying new, 2 items/ year saves £_____ /item (2 x estimated cost of new item)
- ☐ Less dry cleaning, clothes aired outside at night, 1 suit or coat/yr saves £_____ /item (estimate cost)
- ☐ Less photography, buy a post card instead, __ rolls of film/year saves __rolls x ____price= £_____/year

Our Resource and Pollution Inventory

Summarize your household's resource usage and pollution by measuring for a week when you start, and then a year later. Use the measurement methods suggested below, or any measurements from other eco-checklists, or invent your own ways to quantify.

Resource or pollution type	Amount today	Amount later
Rubbish		
Bags per week	_____	_____
Food		
Cans, jars, frozen meals, dried sauces, prepared packages, etc: number bought (or used) per week	_____	_____
Packaged drinks: bottles per week	_____	_____
Food bill: £ per week	_____	_____
Organic foods: number or kilograms bought per week	_____	_____
Laundry, Toiletries and Home Chemicals bottles and packages bought or used during a week, month or year	_____	_____

Resource and Pollution Inventory

Resource or pollution type	Amount today	Amount later
Home Energy		
Heating: £ per month	_____	_____
Electricity: £ per month	_____	_____
Cooking: total minutes per day of use of a burner, oven, microwave or kettle	_____	_____
Washing machine: loads per week	_____	_____
Dryer: minutes of use per week	_____	_____
Lighting: number of lamps lit in the evening	_____	_____
Hot water: number of litres per day	_____	_____
Car and Recreation		
Car miles per week (or year)	_____	_____
Air miles per year (estimate)	_____	_____
Water		
Litres per day (or month)	_____	_____
Stress Indicator		
Nights per week with too little sleep	_____	_____
Days gone by without calling a friend	_____	_____

Afterword

And lest the details of my story seem too many to remember, it all comes down to pointing yourself in the right direction, then taking it one step at a time.

MY BASICS

less RUBBISH

less harmful FOOD (less frozen, less canned,
   less powdered, less bottled drink, less transportation,
   less meat, less fish, etc.)

fewer CHEMICALS

less ENERGY

less WATER

less STRESS

less WEAPONRY and WAR

How each of us lives is important!
Have fun, keep up the good work and good luck!

Further Reading

In other places you can find good extensive lists of practical books on everything from composting to low-energy living to keeping chickens. For broad yet deep educational background about our human predicament in relation to our environment, I recommend these excellent books:

Water: a natural history by Alice Outwater, 1996. Beautifully told history of the environmental degradation of North America by the Europeans beginning in 1500, with water as the unifying theme. How the beaver, bison and prairie dog created moist life habitats, and when they were exterminated, the dust bowl began.

Something New Under the Sun: an environmental history of the twentieth century by John McNeil, 2000. Broad, systematic, extremely thorough and well told history of mankind's re-shaping of the physical world with detailed examples from cities and regions worldwide. Told with a historian's keen eye for the social and political currents behind the events.

Gaia: The practical science of planetary medicine by James Lovelock, 2000 and The Ages of Gaia, 1988. The two billion year history of life on planet Earth, evolving and maintaining itself as an interdependent whole.

Further Reading

So Shall We Reap by Colin Tudge, 2003. Describes agriculture's history as going from local craftsmanship rooted in practical experience and the biology of the earth to large-scale corporate business rooted in money. Describes the efficiency and robustness of mixed animal and crop farms (as in the family farm), and of traditional diets that are high in grains, fruits and vegetables, and low in meat; a diet which he believes will allow our well-being to continue long into the future.

Diet for a Small Planet by Frances Moore Lappé, 1971. Pioneering work on the efficiency of vegetable proteins that feed most of the world. Points out the great resources required for the high meat/fish/fowl diet in modern societies.

The One Straw Revolution by Masanobu Fukuoka, 1985 (This book is difficult to find). Biochemist Fukuoka tells how he began questioning the existing agricultural paradigm, thinking differently, experimenting and gradually developed a new way to farm and live peacefully that was more efficient than modern farmers, using no chemicals and not even a tractor.

Small Is Beautiful, E. F. Schumacher, 1975. Economist Schumacher analyzes and reflects deeply on the globalized economy and the true efficiency of small-scale, local activity to meet our needs and satisfy our hearts, given that we have other values than just money and cheap goods.

Dictionary of Environmental Science and Technology, Andrew Porteous, 2000. Gives solid technical description, background, explanation and data that can be read by both non-technical and technically trained readers.

From Green Books:

Composting for All by Nicky Scott, 2003. Everything you need to know about making your own compost.

Reduce Reuse Recycle by Nicky Scott, 2004. An easy household guide with A-Z of list of household items and how to recycle them.

Cutting Your Car Use by Anna Semlyen, revised edition 2003. A guide to the alternatives for anyone wanting to reduce or eliminate their car use.

Some other books that inspire thinking, reflection and action:

The Man Who Planted Trees by Jean Giono. Fictional story of how one person's action, a little every day, truly made a difference.

Walden by Henry David Thoreau.

The Prophet by Kahlil Gibran.

Non-Violent Resistance and other books by M. K. Gandhi.

Websites of interest

There are many informative and inspirational sites on the web: here are a few to get you started.

Scientific:
www.unep.org United Nations Environment Programme
www.epa.gov Environmental Protection Agency, USA
www.worldwatch.org Worldwatch Institute

Social and Political:
www.focusweb.org Focus on the Global South
www.twnside.org.sg Third World Network
www.wdm.org.uk World Development Movement

Environmental:
www.wwf.org World Wildlife Fund
www.greenpeace.org.uk Greenpeace
www.foe.org.uk Friends of the Earth

Inspiring Individuals:
www.ashoka.org Ashoka Foundation, support for local innovators
www.rightlivelihood.se Right Livelihood Foundation
www.peacepilgrim.org Peace Pilgrim, who worked during her lifetime for world peace through her personal example in daily life.

About the Author

Archie Duncanson trained as a systems engineer, and after twenty years in industry moved into teaching, translating and writing. He self-published the first edition of *Ecology Begins at Home* in 1989, giving many talks on the subject over a number of years. Now living in Stockholm, he is an avid gardener who loves to be outdoors.

Acknowledgements

Thanks to many, many friends whose support helped make the various editions of this book better: Birgitta Arnell, Maria Aschenbrenner, Helen Atkinson, Författares Bokmaskin, Märta Fritz, Lars Gustafsson, Sture Kullberg, Gun Nordin, Helen Nelson, Annika Rucker, Jiri Dostalek Svensson, Ron Watson, Viveca Wikborn, Erik Wåhlin and other friends around the world.

Special thanks to John Elford and Amanda Cuthbert at Green Books who helped bring this edition up to date and make it more widely available and useful.